Jokes & Riddles

Compiled by Eugene Bradley Coco
Illustrated by Jeff Jarka

MCCLANAHAN BOOK COMPANY, INC.

© 1993 McClanahan Book Company, Inc. All rights reserved.
Published by McClanahan Book Company, Inc.
23 West 26th Street, New York, NY 10010

ISBN 1-56293-350-7

What did the broom say to the vacuum cleaner?

"I wish people would stop pushing us around."

Bob: Why is your dog wearing a clock around his neck?

Kurt: Because he's a watch dog.

What goes over your head and under your feet, but doesn't cover your body?

A jump rope.

Why does a fireman wear red suspenders?

To keep his pants up.

Larry: Did you make your bed today, Sam?

Sam: I sure did. But I think it would have been easier if I just bought one.

Why did the girl go outside with her purse open?

She wanted to see if there was any change in the weather.

Alice: I was on TV today.
Nan: That's great. How long were you
on?
**Alice: Not long. When my mother saw me
sitting there, she made me get off right away.**

What's grey, has large ears, and goes squeak-squeak?

An elephant wearing new shoes.

Mrs. Stern: What is this fly doing in my soup?

Waiter: The backstroke.

How does a frog cross a busy street?

He hops on a bus.

Farmer Jones: Who would win if a tomato, a squash and some lettuce had a race?

Farmer Smith: The lettuce would be a 'head,' the squash would be 'stuck in the middle,' and the tomato would have to 'catsup' (catch-up).

How did the farmer mend his pants?

With cabbage patches.

Why do birds fly south for the winter?

Because it's too far to walk.

What has many teeth but never any cavities?

A comb.

"Knock, knock."
"Who's there?"
"Banana."
"Banana who?"
"Knock, knock."
"Who's there?"
"Banana."
"Banana who?"
"Knock, knock."
"Who's there?"
"Orange."
"Orange who?"
"Orange you glad I didn't say banana?"

What kind of shoes can you make from banana peels?

Slippers.

I have a head and a tail but no body. What am I?

A penny.

What did one candle say to the other candle?

"Wanna go out with me tonight?"

What did the bedspread say to the bed?

"Don't move! I've got you covered!"

What did one firecracker say to the other firecracker?

"My Pop's bigger than your Pop."

Chuck: How can I catch a squirrel?

Vic: Just act like a nut and he'll follow you anywhere.

What's gray, has four legs, a tail, a trunk, but is only an inch tall?

A mouse going on vacation.

Why did the boy throw the clock out of the window?

He wanted to see time fly.